Art 2.0 of the Deal: Donald J. Trump Hits the Wall is the cautionary tale of a self-proclaimed "stable genius" and modern day dystopian anti-hero à la Winston in George Orwell's *1984*. The "outsider" President soon proves himself to be unprepared and unfit to deal with a global pandemic that threatens the lives of U.S. citizens. More importantly to this incumbent, the "invisible enemy" endangered Trump's campaign and prospects for reelection.

This art hysterical tour de farce — a portrait of our time — is a GPS through the Twilight Zone, filled with iconic visual *CliffsNotes* mile markers to art history, a reality show president, partisan politics, deals, corruption, the coronavirus pandemic, and a New Normal where life and fact are immeasurably stranger than fiction.

The award-winning illustrator/author, Cathy Hull, skillfully guides readers through the harrowing twists and hairpin turns of the 2020 political landscape, 45's motivations and machinations, and the resulting unintended consequences. Fasten your seatbelt, it's a bumpy ride!

Tired of all the rhetoric, pontification, and analysis? Just kick back and enjoy the artwork. Get the picture?

Art 2.0 of the Deal opens with Trump's acquittal following his impeachment where the author's debut book, *Art 101 of the Deal: Donald J. Trump Off the Wall* left off. It concludes with the ultimate made-for-TV season finale or perhaps series cliffhanger: an uncertain future to be determined by voters in what conspiracy theorists such as POTUS himself call "a rigged election." The inefficiency of the electoral system combined with slow mail delivery during a pandemic are cause for concern; the plot never ceases to thicken. Take a front row seat and view the Trump Show in vivid detail and living color.

Be aware — there is no intermission. This president, in effect, called dibs on the election avowing defeat was neither an option nor a possibility. Stay tuned. See what happens….

Meanwhile, Donald Trump and Cathy Hull continue to be the gift that keeps on giving. Laughter is infectious. Pass it on.

Illustrations and text by Cathy Hull · Layout and design by Lawrence Voigtsberger

ISBN 978-0-578-79892-9

CathyHullOriginals.com

ART 2.0 OF THE DEAL

DONALD J. TRUMP HITS THE WALL

Written and Illustrated by **CATHY HULL**

TOCQUEVILLE PRESS · NEW YORK

"By amusing myself with all these games, all this nonsense,
I am only a public entertainer who has understood his time."
—PABLO PICASSO

I've always felt that a lot of modern art is a con, and that the most successful painters are often better salesmen and promoters than they are artists.
—DONALD J. TRUMP, *The Art of the Deal*

This book is dedicated to Donald J. Trump,
our very own American Machiavelli. Determined to retain
the White House at any cost and uniquely qualified to upstage a
plague, apocalyptic wildfires, floods, storms, and an economic
collapse in the midst of the most exhausting, ideologically
polarized presidential race in American history.

MAGA hats off to you!

"This idea of art for art's sake is a hoax."
–PABLO PICASSO

"Art is not a mirror to hold up to society, but a hammer with which to shape it."
–LEON TROTSKY

"Art is meant to disturb, science reassures."
–GEORGES BRAQUE

"Life doesn't imitate art, it imitates bad television."
–WOODY ALLEN

"Art: cheaper than therapy: and you get pictures."
–CATHY HULL

"Nothing is easy: but who wants nothing?"
–DONALD J. TRUMP

realdonaldtrump

4,573 likes

realdonaldtrump Who knew this innocent kid would grow into a monster? #TBT #Trump

View all 2,288 comments

B.C.

Before Coronavirus

"Well, Donald, you're not in Queens anymore."
—DONALD J. TRUMP

66 *People want to find a meaning in everything and everyone. That's the disease of our age.* **99**
—PABLO PICASSO

The COVID-19 global pandemic ravaging the states, is the definitive litmus test of Donald Trump's unconventional, chaotic leadership and decision making style. In the midst of a tumultuous election year, the self-proclaimed "LAW & ORDER!!!" President is simultaneously plagued with a cratered economy, mass protests against police brutality and institutional racism, while attempting to combat and abort emerging tell-all manuscripts and memoirs. Timing is everything; it's a perfect storm!

"Winning" has always been Trump's mantra, business model, and way of life. This president is unable or unwilling to put the well-being of the American people before his need and desire for a second term. Warning of a rigged election, spreading conspiracy theories, accusing the democrats of using the intelligence agencies to spy on his campaign, "the political crime of the century..." the incumbent is running as an outsider and underdog. Of course, he accepts no responsibility; there is plenty of blame to go around and around.

Rest assured, nevertheless, The Donald never ceases to shock his critics and awe his fans.

Spoiler alert: with his political future uncertain, and a number of congressional and gubernatorial races on the line, Donald J. Trump lets no crisis go to waste, making ample time to mete out retribution to his enemies and reward loyalists with pardons.

The Trump show is live reality TV.

Will it be renewed?

*66 And I think something could happen.
We'll see what happens, but something will happen. 99*
—DONALD J. TRUMP

SURVIVAL OF
THE FITTEST

"If you have them by the balls, their hearts and minds will follow."
—**DONALD J. TRUMP,** quoting (without attribution) Theodore Roosevelt

THE CON ARTIST

Claiming money was never his motivation — except as a way to keep score —
Donald Trump confides that some people paint beautifully on canvas.
But he likes making deals. Preferably big deals. That's how he gets his kicks.

*" Picasso obviously viewed his art as a business, which it was.
I view my business as an art, which it is. "*
—DONALD J. TRUMP

15

HOW DO I LOVE ME?

President Trump basks in the power of his office, seizing the day and spotlight. The self-styled entertainer and showman has maximized the bully pulpit to dominate the news cycle. *Let me count the ways.*

66 *People love me. And you know what,*
I have been very successful. Everybody loves me. 99
—DONALD J. TRUMP

Donald J. Trump ✔
@realDonaldTrump

"Revenge is sweet and not fattening." - Alfred Hitchcock

4:53 PM · Dec 15, 2014   ⓘ

♡ 3.8K   💬 2.1K people are Tweeting about this

WINNING STRATEGIES

A Second Chance to Make a First Impression

FAULT LINES

Trump, a protégé of Roy Cohn, viewed his acquittal as vindication and weaponized it to denounce his enemies and rally his followers. Chaos and fear rule; vengeance is his.

USA TODAY

ACQUITTED

"If an injury has to be done to a man it should be so severe that his vengeance need not be feared."
—MACHIAVELLI

DIVINE COMEDY

Poetic justice and divine retribution. In *Inferno*, the darker your crimes, the lower the levels of hell you descend to until you meet up with Satan himself, trapped at the center of it all. Welcome to the Trump administration.

" *Abandon hope, all ye who enter here.* "
—DANTE

23

NO YOLK

Trump sees himself as a blameless victim — first of the impeachment and then the pandemic. When not bragging or exhibiting false bravado about his successes, he flaunts his "woe-is-me" attitude. It's his party, and he'll cry if he wants to. Often.

66 I think I handled it very well, but I guess it probably did [distract me]. I mean, I got impeached. I think, you know, I certainly devoted a little time to thinking about it, right? I don't think I would have done any better had I not been impeached. Okay? ... I don't think I would have acted any differently or I don't think I would have acted any faster. 99
—DONALD J. TRUMP

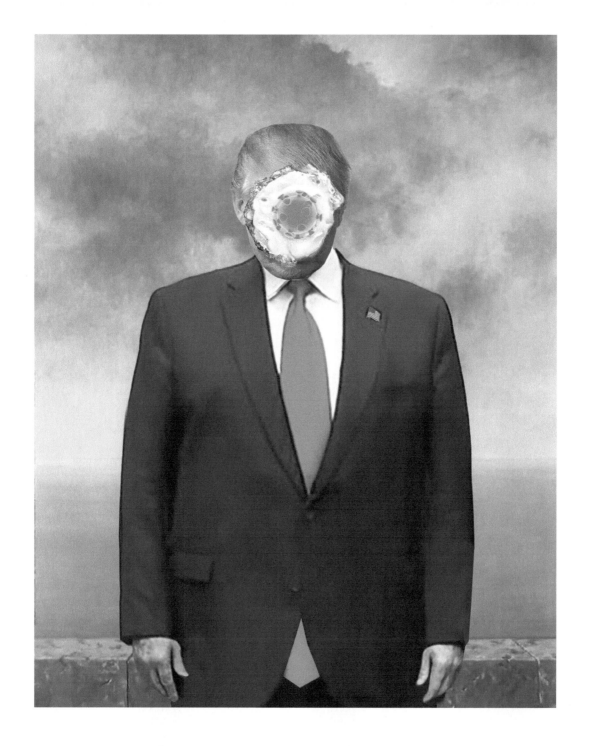

ABOUT FACE

Trump hides in plain sight, reinventing himself and the political playbook on a daily basis. He will contradict himself and reverse course at the drop of a MAGA hat, if it suits his narrative and purpose.

" If you're careful about what you reveal, you'll have more flexibility. "
—DONALD J. TRUMP

THE INVISIBLE ENEMY

Trump's hair, a distracting wonder of the modern world — like his White House — is under siege. Imagine if he had only devoted as much time and attention to the political challenges at hand instead of his coif. How differently he might have dealt with these crises. Hair today. Gone tomorrow?

66 My hair is blowing around. And it's mine. The one thing you cannot get away with. It is a problem if you are president. 99
—DONALD J. TRUMP

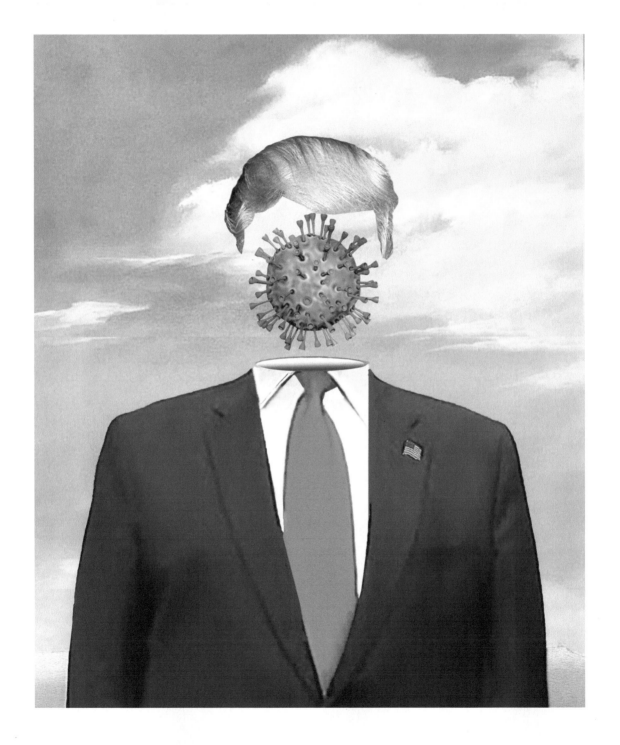

MADE IN CHINA

Get a grip. Trump struggled to raise his falling approval ratings after mishandling the coronavirus threat. True to form, he returned to a familiar pattern: blame the foreigners. Unfortunately, sticks, stones and name-calling the virus the "China plague," "Wuhan virus," and "Kung Flu" is no cure for pandemics and diseases.

66 *We have it totally under control. It's one person coming in from China, and we have it under control. It's going to be just fine.* 99
—DONALD J. TRUMP

THE DEMOCRATIC HOAX

Hillary Clinton remains the personification of the liberal establishment and all that Trump is fighting. Trump is still trying to "LOCK HER UP" and cinch his reelection.

66 The Democrats are politicizing the coronavirus; this is their new hoax. 99
—DONALD J. TRUMP

HINDSIGHT IS 2020

Trump has questioned the science, disputed his experts, and lashed out at studies and doctors that contradicted him with surgical precision.

66 *Sometimes the picture is clearer if you're not in the picture at all.* 99
—DONALD J. TRUMP and ROBERT T. KIYOSAKI from
Why We Want You to Be Rich

THE TRUTH SLAYER

George Washington could not tell a lie. Nixon could not tell the truth.
Trump cannot tell the difference.

*66 I don't know if you've seen, the polls have been going up like a rocket
ship. George Washington would have had a hard time beating me before the
plague came in, before the China plague. 99*
—DONALD J. TRUMP

TOUGH CALL

Truth or Consequences. Don't believe your lying eyes!
The Trump Administration assessed the danger of the oncoming pandemic
and assured America it will go away. There goes the ballgame.

" 'Mr. President, they tried to beat you on Russia, Russia, Russia.'
That didn't work out too well. They couldn't do it. They tried the
impeachment hoax.... They lost ... and this is their new hoax. "
—DONALD J. TRUMP

IDIOT SAVANT

Trump refused to heed the warnings, flouted advice and public health guidelines from experts in his own administration, and failed to warn, prepare, or protect the country. The power of his positive thinking would, in his mind, save us. How's that working out for you so far?

66 *Now, I have to tell you, it's an unbelievably complex subject. Nobody knew health care could be so complicated.* 99
—DONALD J. TRUMP

STROKE OF GENIUS

What's your poison? America drank the Kool-Aid in 2016 — "oh yeaaah!"
Will they drink the bleach in 2020?

*66 Think about it: We live in a world where there are warnings
on bottles of bleach — we have to tell people not to drink bleach.
In that world, Trump can be president. 99*
—RICKY GERVAIS

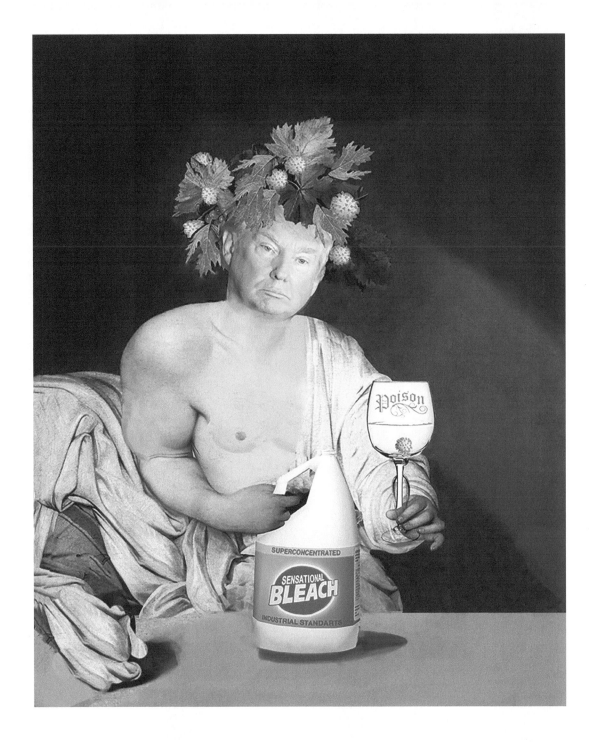

NO BRAINER

Mad as a hatter, the self-proclaimed stable genius "aced" an acuity test
for cognitive impairment, admitting, "I can't remember the name of it."
Trump felt the need to make a clean breast of results to put to rest questions
of his own mental fitness and prove his fortitude and proficiency.
Get the picture?

**"*I got a perfect mark. And the doctors were … they said:
Very few people can do that. Very few people get that. You understand?*"**
—DONALD J. TRUMP

AY CORONA!

Trump is a numbers man obsessed with "Bachelor finale" type ratings, not coronavirus death tolls where the president has indeed made America First.

What separates the winners from the losers is how a person reacts to each new twist of fate.
—DONALD J. TRUMP

GRAVE MISTAKE

Testing … one, two, three. Trump has done his worst to downplay the threat of COVID-19. He liked the numbers where they were; hence, they should slow the testing down. Please.

66 *They — in most — most cases, in almost — I mean, literally, in most cases, they automatically cure. They automatically get better.* **99**
—DONALD J. TRUMP

49

CABIN FEVER

In his inimitable way, Donald Trump called protesters rallying against coronavirus lockdowns — some even threatening the lives of governors — "good people."

❝ *They've got cabin fever. They want their lives back.* ❞
—DONALD J. TRUMP

51

SHOWTIME

Trump is all show and no tell … a political circus. His (mis)handling of the pandemic was catastrophic with dire consequences.

66 You're going to see. I don't want to tell you now, but right now, we have a very strong indication that we know pretty much … we have some good ideas. 99
—DONALD J. TRUMP

TAKING A MULLIGAN

COVID-19 surges and jobless benefits expire. Trump heads to his namesake golf club. (298 times to date.) Par for the course.

66 Actually, I play VERY fast, get a lot of work done on the golf course, and also get a 'tiny' bit of exercise. Not bad!99
—DONALD J. TRUMP

REALITY CHECK PLEASE

Trump's *feel good* assurances to the contrary, America First has new meaning.
The U.S. is doing worse than any other country and has the highest fatality rate.
We passed the mile mark of 255,076* deaths related to the coronavirus,
cementing our global leadership status. How's that for exceptionalism?

66 *The world is not doing well and we're going great.* **99**
—DONALD J. TRUMP

*Death toll at the time of printing

BEATS ME

The brute facts of presidential failure combating this "invisible" enemy simply elude him; he accepts no responsibility. Ever. Will 45's mocking of masks as a culture war issue, his denial and downplaying of the greatest public health crisis in 100 years be reason enough to disqualify him from serving a second term?

" My f***ing generals are a bunch of p***ies. "
—DONALD J. TRUMP

FRUIT OF THE POISONOUS TREE

The Apple Doesn't Fall Far From the Orange

"Friends are good, but family is better."

—DONALD J. TRUMP

THE ROOT OF THE PROBLEM

Trump has marketed his name, his most valuable asset,
and branched out beyond NYC, licensing TRUMP on a plethora of
endeavors including hotels, a brand of vodka, energy drinks in Israel,
a winery in Virginia, steaks, water. Money is no object … it's not his.

*" I've used the laws of this country to pare debt…. We'll have the company.
We'll throw it into a chapter. We'll negotiate with the banks. We'll make a fantastic
deal. You know, it's like on* The Apprentice. *It's not personal. It's just business. "*
—DONALD J. TRUMP

READ MY LIPS

Too close for comfort. Faustian bargain aside,
Melania cannot mask her true feelings.

66 *I've had bad luck with all my wives. The first one left me and the*
second one didn't. The third gave me more children! 99
—DONALD J. TRUMP

DRESSED TO KILL FOR IT

Daddy's little girl and favorite son, Ivanka, was groomed to follow in his footsteps. One of these days those stilettos are gonna walk all over you.

66 *I want to see the first woman president also. They're all saying, 'we want Ivanka.'* 99
—DONALD J. TRUMP

Ivanka Trump
46th President of the United States

YANKEE DOODLE DANDY

Jared added another feather to his cap taking charge of the federal response
to the COVID-19 pandemic. He now instructs the DHHS, CDC, and FDA.
Guess Kushner's previous goal of bringing peace to the Middle East
was not challenging enough.

*66 'Tis a lesson you should heed: If at first you don't succeed, try, try again.
Then quit. There's no use being a damn fool about it. 99*
—W.C. FIELDS

69

SHOOTING BLANKS

It's the same old song. Dad wrote the book — but devoted first son and namesake ripped pages from his father's syllabus with a tome of rants against American liberals. Regardless, Mini Don's inflated book sales and ego were assured by the RNC's pre-release bulk purchase.

Donald Trump Jr. ✓
@DonaldJTrumpJr

Thanks Deplorables! You're the best. Trump Jr's 'Triggered' Debuts At #1 On NYT Best Sellers List - The Daily Caller

8:25 AM · Nov 14, 2019 ⓘ

♡ 33.2K   💬 8.1K people are Tweeting about this

PRIMAL SCREAM

Kimberly Guilfoyle, Trump campaign fundraiser and girlfriend of Donald Trump Jr., yelled a full-throttle, bone-chilling, no-ears-spared endorsement assuring a virtually empty auditorium: "THE BEST IS YET TO COME."
Tympanoplasty?

66 *That was fantastic ... so amazing. So much energy ... so much passion....*
Nobody could have done that, but you, my Kimberly, it was one of the
greatest speeches I have ever seen. 99
—DONALD J. TRUMP

MAN UP

Eric Trump's father is his idol and role model. The president's third child and second son by Ivana may run day-to-day operations of the family real estate empire under Donald's watchful eye — but, clearly, his full-time job is pleasing his dad.

Eric Trump ✓
@EricTrump

#BidensACoward

3:26 PM · Oct 8, 2020

♡ 56.4K   ♡ 23.7K people are Tweeting about this

❝ I think I'll do better. ❞

—DONALD J. TRUMP, comparing his record running the family business to his children's

THE INGENUE

On cue, the oft ignored, rarely-sighted second daughter of Donald Trump dutifully took to the stage and played to an audience of one at the RNC convention offering a passionate plea for her father's reelection.

66 *Study me as much as you like, you will never know me. For I differ a hundred ways from what you see me to be. Put yourself behind my eyes, and see me as I see myself. Because I have chosen to dwell in a place you can't see.* 99

—Quote by RUMI posted to Instagram by TIFFANY TRUMP

THE RELUCTANT BARRON

One could catch a rare glance of Trump's youngest son at the RNC, which clearly was a family affair. Barron, however, leads a distinctly different life from his older siblings. Although he resides at the White House, his father opts to put his elder children in the spotlight instead. Give the devil his due.

" He's like everyone else, he's in his room … he's not as happy as you could be. He'd like to be playing sports. "
—DONALD J. TRUMP

STRANGE BEDFELLOWS

Cats and Dogs

*"Most people want what's best for themselves, not for you.
If those people have already spent a great deal of effort
on their homework, why would they share it with you?"*

—DONALD J. TRUMP

THAT'S BASEBALL

It's a whole new ballgame when Vladimir Putin is involved in U.S. elections and the all-American sport. Donald Trump is out of his league. Keep your eye on the ball.

66 *You put the wrong person in office, you'll see things that you would not have believed are possible.* 99
—DONALD J. TRUMP

THE LADY OF THE HOUSE

No love lost. Trump vs. the Speaker *and Lady* of the House, is an ongoing battle. Under the Constitution, she is a leader of a branch of government equal to the chief executive. Our peerless POTUS has met his match.

 **Donald J. Trump** ✔
@realDonaldTrump

Crazy "Nancy Pelosi, you are a weak person. You are a poor leader. You are the reason America hates career politicians, like yourself." @seanhannity She is totally incompetent & controlled by the Radical Left, a weak and pathetic puppet. Come back to Washington and do your job!

9:33 AM · Apr 16, 2020 ⓘ

♡ 275.8K 💬 125.4K people are Tweeting about this

DÉJÀ VU

Trump and Pence, together again, saddled up for the 2020 election.
Hi Ho, Silver.

Make America Great Again. Again.
—MIKE PENCE

PAS DE DEUX

The Slovenian Sphinx and her spouse like to sway to
Frank Sinatra's "My Way." Trump can't dance. Don't ask him.
Can he lead the country for four more years?

DONALD & MELANIA GAIETY DANCE TEAM

CHEERS AND JEERS

Two, four, six, eight.
Who do they appreciate?
Donald, Donald.
Rah! Rah! Rah!
Gooooooooooooo Dad!

" *Children of successful people are generally very, very troubled, not successful.* "
—DONALD J. TRUMP

WARDROBE MALFUNCTION

Why is it we have seen the First Lady's breasts but not our president's taxes? Despite several unfulfilled promises to do so, Trump continues the fight in the courts to closet them. Just another empty suit?

66 *If I decide to run for office, I will release my tax returns. Absolutely. I would love to do that.* 99
—DONALD J. TRUMP

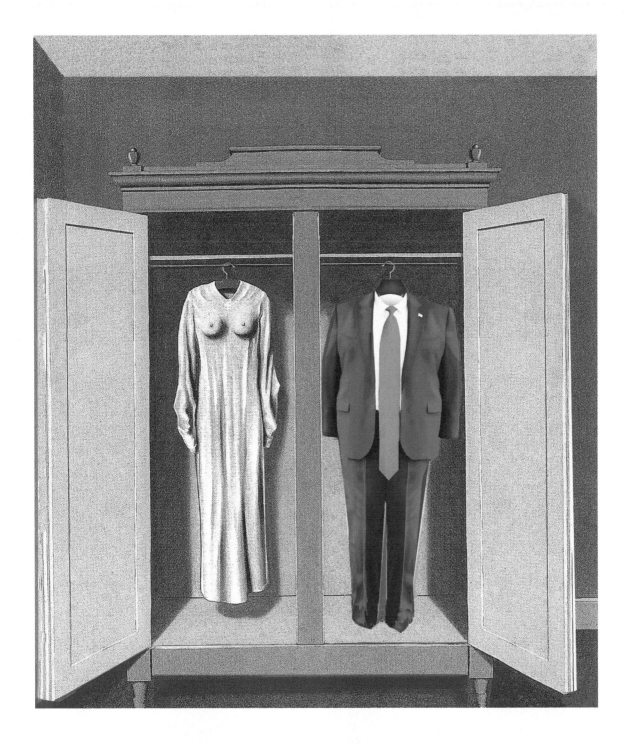

ALL THE PRESIDENT'S MEN (AND WOMEN)

Loyal to a Fault

"The first method for estimating the intelligence of a ruler is to look at the men he has around him."

—MACHIAVELLI

OLLY OLLY OXEN FREE

Vice President Mike Pence takes artistic license painting a very rosy picture of the coronavirus — stating there is no second wave — crediting President Trump, and chastising the media for being alarmist.

" I want the American people to know that from the very first day President Donald Trump has put the health of America first. "
—MIKE PENCE

JUDGE, JURY, AND EXECUTIONER

One nation under Trump with liberty and justice for the select, favored few. William Barr no longer even pretends to defend the law. Trump's legal consigliere remorselessly serves at the pleasure of the president, adeptly tipping the scales of justice to protect 45 at any cost.

66 It may be better to live under robber barons than under omnipotent moral busybodies. 99
—WILLIAM BARR, quoting C.S. Lewis

THE FIX IS IN

Whiplash. Just 46 days before the election, Senate Majority Leader Mitch McConnell and President Trump rushed to fill RBG's seat "without delay" — despite the fact that voting had begun. Damn the torpedoes (and the precedent McConnell set)! Full speed ahead! Eight days before voters go to the polls: Mission Accomplished!

66 *The American people should have a voice in the selection of their next Supreme Court Justice. Therefore, this vacancy should not be filled until we have a new president.* 99
—MITCH MCCONNELL (on the day of Scalia's death)

IT'S MILLER TIME

Stephen Miller, Machiavellian policy adviser to the president, is the behind-the-scenes operator whose various nefarious obsessions have shaped Trump's thinking and agenda.

66 Our opponents, the media, and the whole world will soon see as we begin to take further actions, that the powers of the president to protect our country are very substantial and will not be questioned. 99
—STEPHEN MILLER

DIPLOMATIC IMMUNITY

Pompeo's leadership at the State Department and his Tartuffery as a partisan Trumpist political appointee is always on display. Yet POTUS has buyer's remorse and laments the fact that Pompeo has not done enough to implicate his political opponents. Find Hillary Clinton's 2016 emails. Fetch!

> *They're in the State Department, but Mike Pompeo has been unable to get them out, which is very sad, actually, I'm not happy about him for that reason. He was unable to get them out. I don't know why. You're running the State Department, you get them out.*
> —DONALD J. TRUMP

WHAT ARE THEIR ODD$?

Treasury Secretary Steven Mnuchin reassures small businesses
that he's confident Congress will approve additional funding on top of
the original $350 billion already being distributed. Pipe dream on.

*66 Relative to shutting off the entire economy and relative to people thinking
we would have 40 million unemployed, we are doing great. 99*
—STEVEN MNUCHIN

GOOD FORTUNE

Fairy tales do come true for top Trump adviser Larry Kudlow, director of the White House National Economic Council. He prophesied early on that "This is a Chinese pandemic" and COVID would have "minimal impact" on the U.S. economy. At the RNC convention, he concluded the pandemic was in the past tense on a day the U.S. recorded 1,147 COVID-19 deaths. And he lived happily ever after.

66 Then came a once-in-100-year pandemic. It was awful. Health and economic impacts were tragic. Hardship and heartbreak were everywhere. But presidential leadership came swiftly and effectively with an extraordinary rescue for health and safety to successfully fight the COVID virus. 99
—LARRY KUDLOW

SIGNATURE STYLE

White House coronavirus response coordinator Dr. Deborah Birx, a world-renowned global health official for three-plus decades and key player in HIV/AIDS vaccine research will not be remembered for her reveals at daily White House press briefings; her scarves were her most powerful statements.

 **Donald J. Trump**
@realDonaldTrump

So Crazy Nancy Pelosi said horrible things about Dr. Deborah Birx, going after her because she was too positive on the very good job we are doing on combatting the China Virus, including Vaccines & Therapeutics. In order to counter Nancy, Deborah took the bait & hit us. Pathetic!

9:44 AM · Aug 3, 2020

♡ 98.7K   See the latest COVID-19 information on Twitter

HONORABLE MENTION

Trump is prone to attack his own infectious disease expert,
Dr. Anthony Fauci, refuting his top government adviser's claims
regarding the coronavirus' cause, effect, surge and the U.S. response.

66 Prevention is better than cure. 99
—DESIDERIUS ERASMUS

*66 People are tired of hearing Fauci and all these idiots,
all these idiots who got it wrong. 99*
—DONALD J. TRUMP

A CAPPELLA

Fox News commentators continue to sing Trump's praises and serve as a mouthpiece for his administration, providing "propaganda" and a "feedback loop" for the president. It's the closest we've come to having state TV.

66 *I've told the truth, I didn't come to fool you*
And even though it all went wrong
I'll stand before the Lord of Song
With nothing on my tongue but Hallelujah. 99
—LEONARD COHEN

115

ANYTHING GOES

Testing Trump's coattails, several GOP candidates are off to the races. Senate seats and their state's electoral votes are up for grabs in a high-stakes fight for Senate control. And the presidency. Place your bets....

117

FAKE VIEWS

This press secretary, Kayleigh McEnany, is the ready for primetime, picture-perfect, MAGAnificent model and spokeswoman for Trump's reelection campaign. In keeping with her boss's perpetual denunciations of the media, Kayleigh's orchestrated smackdowns, share-worthy clips, and mic-dropping exits ensure she always gets the last word.

66 When the speech condemns a free press, you are hearing the words of a tyrant. 99
—THOMAS JEFFERSON

Donald J. Trump
@realDonaldTrump

The Coronavirus is very much under control in the USA. We are in contact with everyone and all relevant countries. CDC & World Health have been working hard and very smart. Stock Market starting to look very good to me!

4:42 PM · Feb 24, 2020

 135.7K   ⚡ See the latest COVID-19 information on Twitter

UNINTENDED CONSEQUENCES

Still Life

"History repeats itself, first as tragedy, second as farce."
—KARL MARX

HELP WANTED

The global pandemic has resulted in the largest number of shutdowns and lockdowns worldwide at the same time in history. Welcome to the new normal. Have a nice day!

" I'll be the greatest jobs President that God ever created."
—DONALD J. TRUMP

OUT OF SERVICE

Non-essential shops, bars and restaurants were temporarily closed in March for better or worse. When the pandemic eventually subsides, roughly one-third of the city's 240,000 small businesses may never reopen.

66 We cannot let the cure be worse than the problem itself. 99
—DONALD J. TRUMP

WE ARE THE WORLD

Sheltering alone together is the new normal
when attempting to stop the pandemic.

66 You really want to know what I consider ideal company? A total piece of ass. 99
—DONALD J. TRUMP

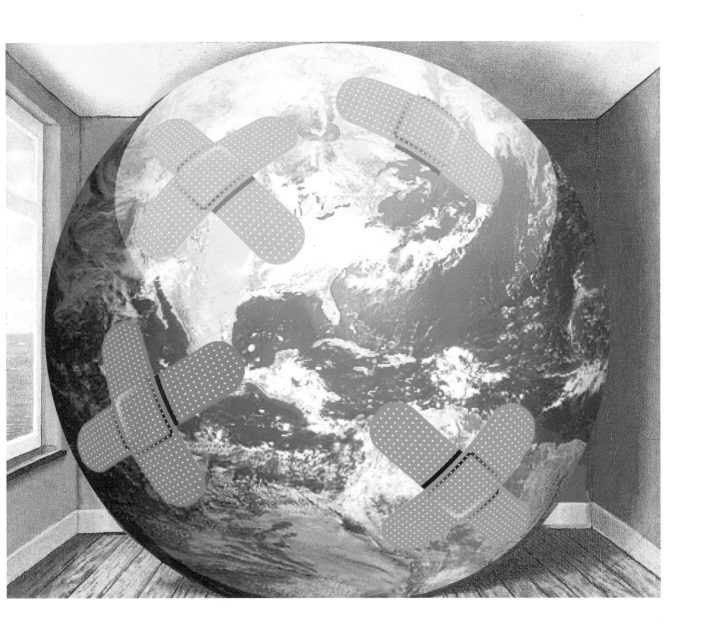

SIGN OF LIFE

Only Trump's learning curve has flattened as he, now a "survivor,"
continues to deny the science and ignore rules his CDC
has put in place to protect the American public.

*66 Please do not take medical advice from a man
who looked directly at a solar eclipse. 99*
—HILLARY CLINTON

MOTHER OF INVENTION

Seniors are considered high-risk candidates for contracting the virus, suffering the most severe symptoms and fatality rates. It is what it is. Hang in there....

66 Now we know it affects elderly people with heart problems and other problems.... If they have other problems, that's what it really affects. That's it. 99
—DONALD J. TRUMP

DIVIDE AND CONQUER

Love him or hate him, Trump — like a train wreck — is riveting to observe making history while working for a 2020 electoral victory. Oh say can't you see?

" You know I'm totally off-script right now.
And this is how I got elected, by being off-script. True. "
—DONALD J. TRUMP

DROIT DU SEIGNEUR

The Royal Treatment

"In the kingdom of the blind, the one-eyed man is king."
—DESIDERIUS ERASMUS

AT YOUR SERVICE

The arrogant TV persona and self-promoting anti-hero with a Napoleonic complex burst onto the political scene like a meteor — breaking all the rules with his unconventional tactics, relentless ambition, and strategic intuition. Will COVID be Trump's Russia?

66 Well, Napoleon finished a little bit bad. 99
—DONALD J. TRUMP

ABSOLUTE POWER TRIPPING

Trump leads with bombast, braggadocio, and the insouciance of a monarch, musing about the Trump dynasty (with Ivanka, heir apparent). It's good to be the King.

66 *He who has the gold makes the rules.* **99**
—DONALD J. TRUMP

PAGEANTRY

And now this: "Cadet Bone Spurs," a five-time draft evader who proclaimed himself *The War President* and protector of confederate monuments, threatened to invoke the Insurrection Act of 1807 and send in the military to maintain law and order.

66 Winning is important, but survival is even more important. If you don't survive, you don't get to fight the next battle. 99
—DONALD J. TRUMP

COMMEDIA DELL'ARTE

Craving the spotlight, adoration, and playing to his base, Trump ignored the COVID-19 epidemic as well as CDC guidelines and doubled down on his culture war to dominate the stage. What so proudly he rails at the twilight's last gleaming. Campaign 2020: the show must go on-and-on and on.

66 We can have a lot of fun tonight. I have nothing to do. Nothing. Nothing. 99
—DONALD J. TRUMP

143

NOBODY'S FOOL

The Devil is in the details. In his parallel universe, Trump is indeed a wild card. Some people live in a dream world, others face reality. 45 turns one into the other.

66 Avoid your comfort zone — it's probably outdated anyway. 99
—DONALD J. TRUMP

145

Donald J. Trump ✔
@realDonaldTrump

...And I had to put up with these losers and still run a Country, AND VERY WELL!

🖼️ **Louie Gohmert** ✔ @replouiegohmert

What I have accumulated here is absolutely shocking upon the realization that #Mueller's disreputable, twisted history speaks to the character of the man placed in a position to attempt to legalize a coup against a lawfully-elected President. DOWNLOAD: hannity.com/media-room/goh...

8:53 AM · Oct 7, 2020   ⓘ

♡ 49K   💬 18.8K people are Tweeting about this

STICK TO YOUR GUNS

In the Crosshairs

"Every time I speak of the haters and losers I do so with great love and affection. They cannot help the fact that they were born fucked up!"
—DONALD J. TRUMP

NASTY WOMAN

Donald Trump never forgives or forgets his nemesis, "Crooked" Hillary Clinton. She is always on his mind and continues to obsess him.

66 I'm living rent-free inside of Donald Trump's brain, and it's not a very nice place to be, I can tell you that.99
—HILLARY CLINTON

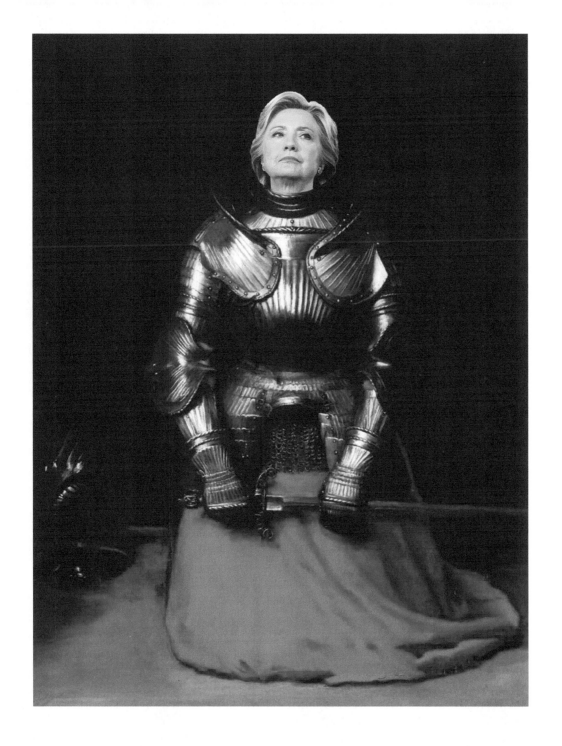

L'ENFANT TERRIBLE

45 tweeted mercilessly mocking and denigrating 16 year old Greta Thunberg, climate and environmental activist and *Time* magazine's Person of the Year 57 years his junior. Hell hath no fury like a petulant man-child scorned and passed over!

66 *So ridiculous. Greta must work on her anger management problem, then go to a good old fashioned movie with a friend! Chill Greta, chill!* 99
—DONALD J. TRUMP

COVER GIRL

Congresswoman Ayanna Pressley, member of the "Squad", is making peace with going bald due to alopecia. She brushes off Hair Führer's racist tweets and fights for a more equitable and just world while Trump takes Propecia and works hard to hide male-pattern hair loss.

Because my hair, I don't know about you, but it has to be perfect. Perfect.
—DONALD J. TRUMP

STATE OF EMERGENCY

Trump's ever expanding number of love-hate relationships and attacks are no longer reserved for specific people but now include entire demographics.

66 Leave Democrat cities. Let them rot. 99
—DONALD J. TRUMP

155

DON'T SHOOT THE MESSENGER

Red Blood, White Privilege, Blue Wall, American Dream, Black Nightmare. Trump is a self-styled arsonist. This president's inflammatory rhetoric encouraged white supremacists adding fuel to the fire.

Donald J. Trump ✔ @realDonaldTrump · May 29, 2020

I can't stand back & watch this happen to a great American City, Minneapolis. A total lack of leadership. Either the very weak Radical Left Mayor, Jacob Frey, get his act together and bring the City under control, or I will send in the National Guard & get the job done right.....

Donald J. Trump ✔
@realDonaldTrump

....These THUGS are dishonoring the memory of George Floyd, and I won't let that happen. Just spoke to Governor Tim Walz and told him that the Military is with him all the way. Any difficulty and we will assume control but, when the looting starts, the shooting starts. Thank you!

12:53 AM · May 29, 2020

♡   See Donald J. Trump's other Tweets

❝ If you want a vision of the future, imagine a boot stamping on a human face — forever. ❞
—GEORGE ORWELL

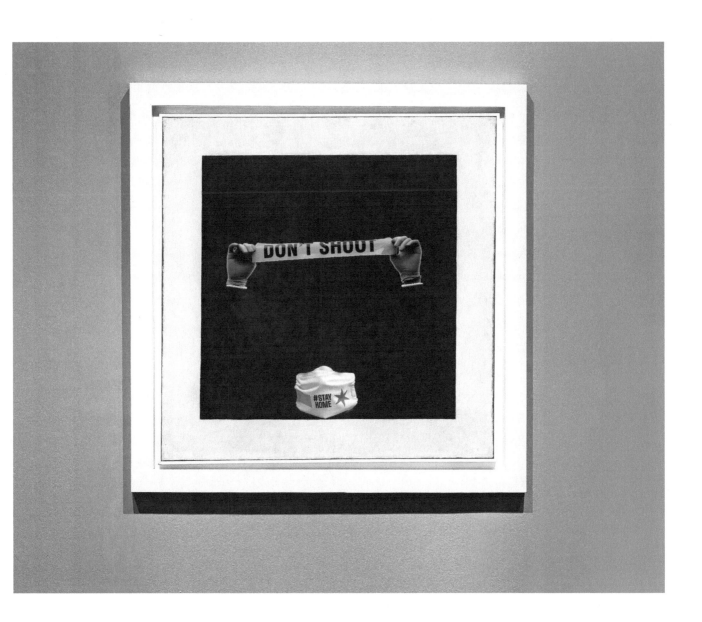

Donald J. Trump
@realDonaldTrump

About the only way a person is able to write a book on me is if they agree that it will contain as much bad "stuff" as possible, much of which is lies. It's like getting a job with CNN or MSDNC and saying that "President Trump is great." You have ZERO chance. FAKE NEWS!

11:35 AM · Aug 29, 2020   ⓘ

♡ 83.7K   💬 35.3K people are Tweeting about this

FULL DISCLOSURE

Do Tell All

"Is this a dagger which I see before me … Or art thou but/a dagger of the mind."
—WILLIAM SHAKESPEARE, *Macbeth*

ET TU, BOLTON?

Despite non-disclosure agreements, restraining orders, and attempts to stop publication, Trump is the topic du jour of several tell-all books. Former National Security advisor John Bolton's *The Room Where it Happened* details why he believes Trump is unfit for office.

Donald J. Trump ✓
@realDonaldTrump

Wacko John Bolton's "exceedingly tedious" (New York Times) book is made up of lies & fake stories. Said all good about me, in print, until the day I fired him. A disgruntled boring fool who only wanted to go to war. Never had a clue, was ostracized & happily dumped. What a dope!

12:10 AM · Jun 18, 2020   ⓘ

♡ 139.7K   💬 75.4K people are Tweeting about this

161

CLOAK AND DAGGERS

Do kiss and tell-all. The Trump Administration's efforts to censor speech that reflects negatively on the president or his Administration once again failed. *Disloyal: A Memoir*, written by Michael Cohen, Trump's former fixer, gives a stark analysis of Individual 1. Cohen may have lost his moral compass working for the "Boss," but apparently Trump never had one.

" *Michael Cohen's book is fan fiction.* "
—DONALD J. TRUMP

MARY, MARY, QUITE CONTRARY

Mad-as-hell-and-not-going-to-take-it-anymore Mary Trump,
niece to the president and clinical psychologist, writes a tell-all book,
Too Much and Never Enough, about a conspiracy spearheaded by Trump to
defraud her and her brother. A civil lawsuit is pending to hold the family
accountable and recover her rightful inheritance. Karma's a b*tch!

66 *An unstable niece, who was now rightfully shunned, scorned and mocked her
entire life, and never even liked by her own very kind and caring grandfather!* 99
—DONALD J. TRUMP

PITCH PERFECT

Here comes da judge! Maryanne Trump Barry, elder sister
to Donald J. Trump and retired United States Circuit Judge,
candidly spoke out in fifteen hours of face-to-face conversations
(secretly recorded) with and by her niece and author, Mary Trump.

66 *All he wants to do is appeal to his base, He has no principles.
None. None. And his base, I mean my God, if you were a religious
person, you want to help people. Not do this.* 99
—MARYANNE TRUMP BARRY

ALL THE RAGE

Bob Woodward mined pure gold by allowing Trump to be *Trump*.
The president is his own "Deep Throat" boasting that he intentionally played
down the seriousness of the coronavirus at the beginning of the pandemic to
avoid public panic. When asked why, he stated he actually *up*-played it. Got it?

66 *FAKE NEWS! Social pretenders like Bob Woodward,*
who never has anything good to say. 99
—DONALD J. TRUMP

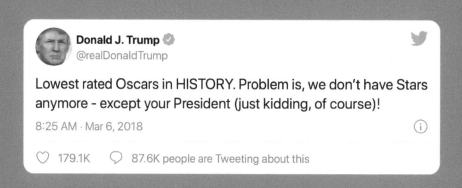

Donald J. Trump ✔
@realDonaldTrump

Lowest rated Oscars in HISTORY. Problem is, we don't have Stars anymore - except your President (just kidding, of course)!

8:25 AM · Mar 6, 2018

♡ 179.1K   💬 87.6K people are Tweeting about this

"I don't kid. Let me just tell you. Let me make it clear."

—DONALD J. TRUMP

COLLATERAL DAMAGE

Cause, Effect, and Photo Ops

"One death is a tragedy; one million is a statistic."
—JOSEF STALIN

"We can learn from our mistakes, but it's better to learn from our successes."
—DONALD J. TRUMP

LAW AND DISORDER

The LAW & ORDER president brought heavily armed soldiers to D.C. and threatened to deploy them nationwide. "Might makes right" has been Trump's modus operandi in his business life and now in his administration. Promises kept; promises broken.

Donald J. Trump ✓
@realDonaldTrump

D.C. had no problems last night. Many arrests. Great job done by all. Overwhelming force. Domination. Likewise, Minneapolis was great (thank you President Trump!).

9:19 AM · Jun 2, 2020 ⓘ

♡ 229.5K 💬 102.6K people are Tweeting about this

DOLLARS AND SENSE

Appearances and bromides are designed to delight and deceive.
Ivanka is a shrewd, calculating political operator loyal to her father.
Her polished demeanor cannot mask naked ambition. She keeps her eyes on
the prize and the keys to the kingdom whether or not it passes the smell test.

*66 You know who's one of the great beauties of the world,
according to everybody? And I helped create her. Ivanka.
My daughter, Ivanka. She's 6 feet tall, she's got the best body. 99*
—DONALD J. TRUMP

LOCATION, LOCATION, LOCATION

Misleading by example. Ivanka Trump encouraged Americans to follow federal guidelines about social distancing advising against discretionary travel before departing with her family for Trump National Golf Club in New Jersey to celebrate the first night of Passover. Dayanu.

66 *Each and every one of us plays a role in slowing the spread.* 99
—IVANKA TRUMP

DRINKING PROBLEM

Trump mercilessly mocked "Little Marco" Rubio for repeatedly sipping from a water bottle. He boasts about his stamina and insists he is in perfect health yet has had difficulty lifting a glass with one hand and seemed unable to guide it all the way up to his lips. Watergate 2020?

66 *I look down at my tie because I've done it, I've taken water and spilled down onto your tie, it doesn't look good for a long time, and frankly the tie is never the same.* 99
—DONALD J. TRUMP

HARD SELL

Ivanka is full of beans. Like father (from the resolute desk) like daughter, both shamelessly violated ethics rules barring government officials from using their public office to endorse specific products or groups for political benefit. POTUS prepares to pass the baton and sharpie.

ETCHED IN STONE

Donald Trump granted executive clemency to longtime friend and adviser
Roger Stone, commuted the veteran Republican operative's prison term,
spared him a hefty fine and two years of supervised release — leaving no
Stone unturned to hedge his bets and insure his re-election.

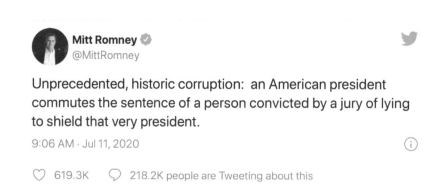

Mitt Romney ✓
@MittRomney

Unprecedented, historic corruption: an American president
commutes the sentence of a person convicted by a jury of lying
to shield that very president.

9:06 AM · Jul 11, 2020

♡ 619.3K   ♡ 218.2K people are Tweeting about this

GO FUND ME

On-again, off-again friend and former advisor, "Sloppy" Steve Bannon, was charged with defrauding donors to a private fund-raising effort, "We Build the Wall," intended to bolster the president's signature initiative along the Mexican border. The bucks stopped here.

66 *When I read about it, I didn't like it. I said this is for the government, this isn't for private people. And it sounded to me like showboating.* 99
—DONALD J. TRUMP

VIRTVTVM &
OMNIVM
VAS

VITIA VIRT
VTI SVBIA
CENT

185

PARDON ME

As women celebrated the centennial of the 19th Amendment, the president who has been repeatedly accused of denigrating women, sexual harassment, assault — even rape — tried to close the gender gap. Multi-tasking, POTUS posthumously pardoned suffragist, Susan B. Anthony, targeting the 2020 Election in the midst of his attacks on mail-in voting.

66 Did you know that … she was never pardoned? What took so long?
And you know that she got a pardon for a lot of other women.
And she didn't put her name on the list. So she was never pardoned. 99
—DONALD J. TRUMP

"Objection! Mr. President!"
The suffragist museum rejected the pardon from President Trump citing voter suppression.

NO TRUTH WITHOUT RUTH

The gloves are off. Only in Donald Trump's America. Before one could say *thank you* or *R.I.P.*, an impeached president nominated a pro-life religious conservative Supreme Court Justice to fill the vacancy created by the death of a beloved liberal feminist icon and gender equality pioneer for a lifetime appointment shortly before a consequential election at warp speed.

Oh come all ye faithful….

66 My most fervent wish is that I will not be replaced until a new president is installed. 99

—RBG

189

COVID CLASSICS

Inside Jokes

"To-morrow, and to-morrow, and to-morrow,
Creeps in this petty pace from day to day."
—WILLIAM SHAKESPEARE, *Macbeth*

THE ART OF DENIAL

Finding creative ways to celebrate the traditional start of summer in the midst of social distancing, lockdowns, and coronavirus alarm.

"But what does it mean, the plague? It's life, that's all."
—ALBERT CAMUS, *The Plague*

TIME IN A BOTTLE

Isolation and quarantine orders. A teetotaling president, partisan politics, and the virus are driving people to drink.

❝ I never had a glass of alcohol. I never had alcohol, for whatever reason. Can you imagine if I had? What a mess I would be. I would be the world's worst. I never drank, OK?❞
—DONALD J. TRUMP

DIRTY MARTINI UP

DWI: drawing while intoxicated. *The ultimate quarantini:*
one part pandemic, one part politics, Trump straight up, no garnish.
Shaken not stirred.

66 Alone, adj. In bad company. 99
—AMBROSE BIERCE

LOCKED AND LOADED

I once spent a year in my apartment, I think it was on a Sunday.

66 *There are days when solitude is a heady wine that intoxicates you with freedom, others when it is a bitter tonic, and still others when it is a poison that makes you beat your head against the wall.* 99
—SIDONIE GABRIELLE COLETTE

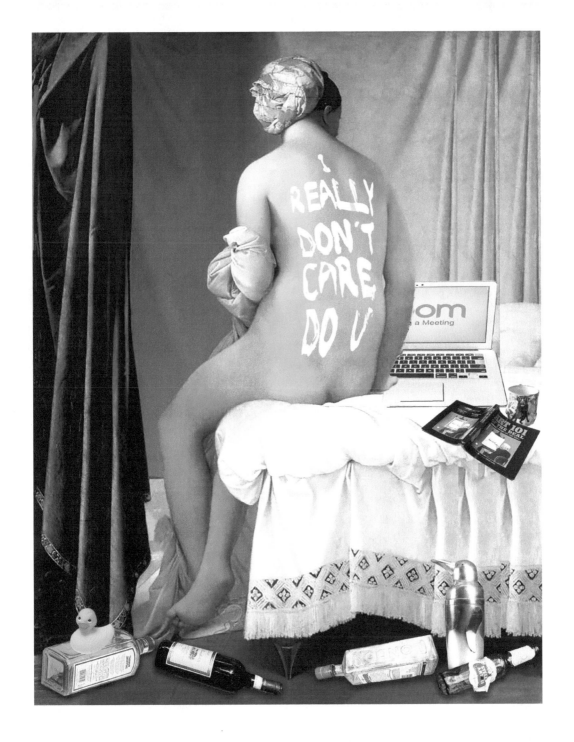

$YMPATHY FOR THE DEVIL

Cognitive dissonance, facts, and figures. The reveal: President Donald Trump paid $0 in federal income tax in ten of the previous fifteen years (including 2014 and 2015), $130K to Stormy Daniels, $200K in taxes to China and has a secret Chinese bank account for licensing deals, $750 in federal taxes (2016 and 2017), owes more than $1 billion in debt, more than $70K (claimed as expenses) to style his hair for TV, and $90K for Ivanka's hair and makeup. The American people have no time or money to dye and learn to embrace and accept their authentic selves.

66 The budget was unlimited, but I exceeded it. 99
—DONALD J. TRUMP

DO THE MATH

Death toll rising, guidelines, warnings, predictions, second wave,
fear of a Twindemic, manic assurances by Patient Zero — a.k.a.
Individual 1 — that COVID is not so bad and shouldn't dominate
your life. Ten days into a standard two-week quarantine, POTUS
returns to the campaign trail. Give us a break … time out!

> *66 All I maintain is that on this earth there are pestilences and there are victims,
> and it's up to us, so far as possible, not to join forces with the pestilences.* 99
> —ALBERT CAMUS, *The Plague*

HITTING THE FAN
...AND THE WALL

Race to the Finish Line

"And he [Biden] is going to be president because some people don't love me, maybe. And all I'm doing is doing my job."
—DONALD J. TRUMP

SUIT UP

Obama has no need to take the measure of the man who was his former V.P. — Joe Biden is tailor made for the 2020 election. Fitting.

Donald J. Trump ✔
@realDonaldTrump

Now @FoxNews is playing Obama's no crowd, fake speech for Biden, a man he could barely endorse because he couldn't believe he won. Also, I PREPAID many Millions of Dollars in Taxes.

12:28 PM · Oct 27, 2020

♡ 111.5K   ○ 53.9K people are Tweeting about this

PLAN A

Joe Biden is ready, willing, and able on day one to build back better than ever!

 *I did more in 47 months as president than Joe Biden did in 47 years.* **—DONALD J. TRUMP**

THAT'S THE TICKET

Way to go! Joe Biden has chosen Kamala Harris to be his V.P. and running mate. The daughter of proud immigrants, a mother from India and father from Jamaica — Kamala was raised to take action.

66 *You may be the first to do many things, but make sure you are not the last.* 99
—KAMALA HARRIS, quoting her mother Shyamala Gopalan Harris

1776

BETWEEN A ROCK AND A HARD PLACE

Mixed messages and double standards. Trump and members of his administration have voted by mail yet fight efforts to expand the practice to the American people warning of a rigged election and fraud.

66 So send it in early and then go and vote. You can't let them take your vote away; these people are playing dirty politics. So if you have an absentee ballot ... you send it in, but I'd check it, follow it and go vote. 99
—DONALD J. TRUMP

FROM SEA TO SHINING SEA

The larger than life Baby Trump Blimp, a globally recognized symbol of opposition, has become ubiquitous in protest of his outsized ego, temperament, and presidency.

66 *Every joke is a tiny revolution.* 99
—GEORGE ORWELL

Inflatable Baby Trump, 2018. Designed and created by Matt Bonner.

THAT'S DEBATABLE

Off the rails. The norm-shattering up-close-and-personal first Presidential debate was widely panned as an embarrassing debacle. Trump, in attack mode, went on a verbal rampage. Neither his opponent nor the moderator, Chris Wallace, was allowed to speak, complete a question or answer. Occasionally, Biden responded in (un)kind. *Stand back and stand by* to be appalled; more "debates" to follow.

*66 I thought the debate last night was great....
We've gotten tremendous reviews on it. 99*
—DONALD J. TRUMP

LIVE AND LET DIE

Who is that unmasked man? Trump is not the president who got America
safely through the COVID-19 pandemic, but he likes to play one on TV.
He rarely wore a mask before contracting the virus and ridiculed his
opponent for doing so, warning the Dems are "telling you what to wear."

*66 Every time you see him, he's got a mask. He could be speaking 200 feet
away from it. And he shows up with the biggest mask I've ever seen. 99*
—DONALD J. TRUMP

RECALCULATING

Uncharted territory. There is no playbook for what to do when the Commander in Chief and leader of the Republican party catches the "Democratic hoax" virus and is hospitalized a month before the election. This campaign is uniquely dependent on this president and candidate; he is the messenger and the message. Trailing in the polls, Trump executes Plan B.

66 *Why don't you drive them crazy and go 16 more years? You'll drive them crazy.* 99
—DONALD J. TRUMP

REIN IN DELUSIONS

Trump must win, win, win at any cost. He is prepared to lose American lives, not the 2020 election. Ostensibly still infectious and not out of the woods, POTUS left Walter Reed National Military Medical Center after admission and emergency treatment for COVID-19 (three days later). Flouting public health guidelines, the "survivor" triumphantly returned to the White House, doubled down on reckless practices, and minimized the coronavirus.

**" *Don't be afraid of COVID. Don't let it dominate your life.…*
We have developed, under the Trump Administration, some really great
drugs and knowledge. I feel better than I did 20 years ago! "**
—DONALD J. TRUMP

THE PUNTER

The White House stonewalled questions regarding the president's present condition and testing results citing HIPAA rules and regulations. On cue, Donald J. Trump, now touting first-hand experience fighting the virus that Biden does not have, takes his COVID show on the road seeming not to realize or care about the lives he could be jeopardizing with his return to the campaign trail.

66 Now they say I'm immune. I feel so powerful. I'll walk in there, I'll kiss everyone in that audience. I'll kiss the guys and the beautiful women, just give you a big fat kiss. 99
—DONALD J. TRUMP

BYE DON

2016 redux. The president refused to commit to a peaceful transition of power should he lose the viral election this November. Amid flaring tempers, fear, and rising gun sales, Trump called for an army of "poll watchers" to monitor the vote. It's time to call it a day. Will this party ever be over…?

66 Well, we're going to have to see what happens. You know that. I've been complaining very strongly about the ballots. And the ballots are a disaster…. We want to have — get rid of the ballots and you'll have a very trans- — we'll have a very peaceful — there won't be a transfer, frankly; there'll be a continuation. The ballots are out of control. You know it. 99

—DONALD J. TRUMP

227

TRUMP

"Two Paths diverged in the woods.
America chose the psychopath."
—PROTEST SIGN

"Washington has not changed Donald Trump —
Donald Trump has changed Washington."
—IVANKA TRUMP

"I wouldn't believe Donald Trump
if he had his tongue notarized."
—ED KOCH

"One who deceives will always find those
who allow themselves to be deceived."
—NICCOLO MACHIAVELLI

"There have been as many plagues
as wars in history; yet always plagues and
wars take people equally by surprise."
—ALBERT CAMUS, *The Plague*

"I think this was a blessing
from God that I caught it."
—DONALD J. TRUMP

TRUMP

"Suburban women, will you please like me?
I saved your damn neighborhood."
—DONALD J. TRUMP

"Out, out, brief candle. Life's but a
walking shadow, a poor player that struts
and frets his hour upon the stage"
—SHAKESPEARE, *Macbeth*

"I'm running against the single worst candidate
in the history of American presidential politics
and you know what that does? That puts
more pressure on me. Can you imagine
if you lose to a guy like this?"
—DONALD J. TRUMP

"History is the judge — its
executioner the proletarian."
—KARL MARX

"Here's the bottom line, I've been very unfairly
treated, and I don't say that as paranoid.
I've been very — everybody says it."
—DONALD J. TRUMP

Schitt$ Creek Season 6 begins

EPITAPH

COVID, COVID, COVID

"I'm one of those folks, or competitors, it's not over till the bell rings."
—JOE BIDEN

"I know that, whatever happens, I'm a survivor — a survivor of success, which is a very rare thing indeed."
—DONALD TRUMP

"Now this is not the end. It is not even the beginning of the end. But it is, perhaps, the end of the beginning."
—WINSTON CHURCHILL

IMAGE REFERENCES

Cover THE EXHIBITIONIST / Back Cover HIGH MAINTENANCE Norman Rockwell. The Picture Hanger or Museum Worker. 1946. Norman Rockwell Museum, Stockbridge, MA, USA.

10 THE OXYMORON Johannes Vermeer. The Astronomer. c. 1668, oil on canvas. The Louvre, Paris, France.

15 THE CON ARTIST Vicente López Portaña. Portrait of Goya. 1826, oil on canvas. Museo del Prado, Madrid, Spain.

17 HOW DO I LOVE ME Caravaggio. Narcissus. c. 1597–1599, oil on canvas. Galleria Nazionale d'Arte Antica in Rome, Italy.

20-21 FAULT LINES Jacques-Louis David. The Death of Socrates. 1787, oil on canvas. Metropolitan Museum of Art, New York, NY, USA.

23 THE DIVINE COMEDY Bronzino. Allegorical Portrait of Dante. 1530, oil on wood. Italian Cultural Institute in New York, NY, USA.

25 NO YOLK René Magritte. The Son of Man. 1946, oil on canvas. Private collection.

27 ABOUT FACE René Magritte. Social Construction of Reality.

29 THE INVISIBLE ENEMY René Magritte. Le Paysage de Baucis. 1966, oil on canvas. Menil Collection, Houston, Texas, USA.

31 MADE IN CHINA Michelangelo. The Creation of Adam. 1508–1512. Sistine Chapel, Rome, Italy.

33 THE DEMOCRATIC HOAX René Magritte. Ready-Made Bouquet. 1956, oil on canvas. Private Collection.

35 HINDSIGHT IS 2020 Norman Rockwell. The Connoisseur. 1962, oil on canvas. Private Collection

37 THE TRUTH SLAYER Gilbert Stuart. George Washington. 1821. National Gallery of Art Washington D.C., USA.

39 TOUGH CALL Norman Rockwell. Game Called Because of Rain, Bottom of the Sixth, or The Three Umpires. 1949. National Baseball Hall of Fame.

41 IDIOT SAVANT Charles Mellin. Portrait of a Gentleman. 1645. Museo de Arte de Ponce, Ponce, Puerto Rico.

43 STROKE OF GENIUS Caravaggio. Bacchus. 1596. Uffizi, Florence, Italy

45 NO BRAINER Quentin Matsys. A Grotesque Old Woman. 1513, oil on oak panel. National Gallery, London, England.

46-47 AY CORONA! Édouard Manet. Dead Toreador. 1864, oil on canvas. National Gallery of Art, Washington, D.C., USA.

49 GRAVE MISTAKE René Magritte. Perspective: Madame Recamier by David. 1949, oil on canvas. Private collection.

51 CABIN FEVER Norman Rockwell. Fifteen Below (Man Reading a Thermometer). Saturday Evening Post Cover, June 29, 1957.

53 SHOWTIME Nicolas Poussin. Hannibal Crossing the Alps on an Elephant. c. 1625. The National Gallery, London, England.

55 TAKING A MULLIGAN Norman Rockwell. The Golfer. c. 1920. Oil on canvas. Norman Rockwell Museum. Stockbridge, MA, USA.

57 REALITY CHECK PLEASE René Magritte. Manet's Balcony. 1950, oil on canvas. Museum of Fine Arts, Ghent, Belgium.

59 BEATS ME Vasily Vereshchagin. Napoleon on the Borodino Heights Napoleon in Russia. 1897. State Historical Museum, Moscow, Russia.

63 THE ROOT OF THE PROBLEM René Magritte. La Folie Almayer (Almayer's Folly). 1951, oil on canvas. Private collection.

65 READ MY LIPS Sebastiano del Piombo. Vittoria Colonna. 1520–1525. Museo Nacional D'Art de Catalunya.

67 DRESSED TO KILL FOR IT Frank Cadogan Cowper. Vanity. 1907. The Royal Academy Collection, London, UK.

69 YANKEE DOODLE DANDY Rembrandt Harmensz van Rijn. An Old Man in Military Costume. c. 1630–1631, oil on panel. J. Paul Getty Museum, Los Angeles, CA, USA.

71 SHOOTING BLANKS Édouard Manet. The Spanish Singer. 1860. Metropolitan Museum of Art, New York, NY, USA.

73 PRIMAL SCREAM Caravaggio. Medusa. 1597, oil on canvas. Uffizi, Florence, Italy.

75 MAN UP Norman Rockwell. The Champ, or, Be a Man. The Saturday Evening Post cover, published April 29, 1922.

77 THE INGENUE Édouard Manet. Plum Brandy. 1877, oil on canvas. National Gallery of Art, Washington, D.C., USA.

79 THE RELUCTANT BARRON Angelo Bronzino. Portrait of a Young Man. 1550–1555, oil on panel. The National Gallery, London, England.

83 THAT'S BASEBALL Norman Rockwell. The Windup. 1939. Norman Rockwell Museum, Stockbridge, MA, USA.

85 THE LADY OF THE HOUSE Norman Rockwell. New Calendar. 1955. Norman Rockwell Museum, Stockbridge, MA, USA.

87 DÉJÀ VU Norman Rockwell. Rocking Horse, 1933. Norman Rockwell Museum, Stockbridge, MA, USA.

89 PAS DE DEUX Norman Rockwell. Gaiety Dance Team. 1937. Private Collection.

91 CHEERS AND JEERS Sam Brown. Cheerleaders. Saturday Evening Post Cover, October 18, 1930.

93 WARDROBE MALFUNCTION René Magritte. Hommage to Mark Sennett. 1934, oil on canvas. Minneapolis Institute Of Art, Minneapolis, MN, USA.

97 OLLY OLLY OXEN FREE Édouard Manet. The Tragic Actor, Rouvière as Hamlet. 1866. Philadelphia Museum of Art, Philadelphia, PA, USA.

99 JUDGE, JURY, AND EXECUTIONER Paul Delaroche. The Execution of Lady Jane Grey 1833, oil on canvas. The National Gallery, London, England.

101 THE FIX IS IN Stuart Gilbert. Catherine Brass Yates (Mrs. Richard Yates). 1793–1794 , oil on canvas.

103 IT'S MILLER TIME Agnolo Bronzino. Portrait of a Young Man With a Book. 1530, oil on board. Metropolitan Museum of Art, New York, NY, USA.

105 DIPLOMATIC IMMUNITY Frans Hals. Willem Heythuijsen. 1634, oil on oak panel. Private collection.

107 WHAT ARE THEIR ODD$? Jacopao de' Barbari. Luca Pacioli. c. 1495–1500, tempera on panel. Capodimonte Museum, Naples, Italy.

109 GOOD FORTUNE Holbein the Younger. Sir Thomas More Hans. 1527, oil on oak. Frick Collection, New York, NY, USA.

111 SIGNATURE STYLE Jean-Auguste-Dominique Ingres. Madame Gonse. 1852, oil on canvas. Musée Ingres, Montauban, France.

113 HONORABLE MENTION Norman Rockwell. I Will Do My Best. 1945. Saturday Evening Post.

115 A CAPPELLA Norman Rockwell. Barbershop Quartet. The Saturday Evening Post cover, September 26, 1936.

117 ANYTHING GOES Georges de la Tour. The Fortune Teller. 1630, oil on canvas. Metropolitan Museum of Art, New York, NY, USA.

119 FAKE VIEWS Ramon Casas i Carbó. After the Ball (Decadence). 1899, oil on canvas. Museum of Montserrat, Barcelona, Spain.

122-123 HELP WANTED Edward Hopper. Early Sunday Morning. 1930, oil on canvas. Whitney Museum, New York, NY, USA.

125 OUT OF SERVICE Vincent van Gogh. Night Café. 1888. Yale University Art Gallery, New Haven, CT, USA.

127 WE ARE THE WORLD René Magritte. The Listening Room. 1952, oil on canvas. Menil Collection, Houston, TX, USA.

129 SIGN OF LIFE Claude Monet. Road Near Giverny. 1885, oil on canvas. Private collection.

131 MOTHER OF INVENTION James McNeill Whistler. Whistler's Mother. 1871. Musée d'Orsay, Paris, France.

133 DIVIDE AND CONQUER Norman Rockwell. Rosie the Riveter. 1943, oil on canvas. Private collection.

137 AT YOUR SERVICE Édouard Detaille. Napoleon in 1806. c. 1912, oil on canvas. Metropolitan Museum of Art, New York, NY, USA.

139 ABSOLUTE POWER TRIPPING Hyacinthe Rigaud. Portrait of Louis XIV. c. 1701, oil on canvas. J. Paul Getty Museum, Los Angeles, CA, USA.

141 PAGEANTRY Charles Wilson Peale. George Washington. c. 1780–1782, oil on canvas. Metropolitan Museum of Art, New York, NY, USA.

143 COMMEDIA DELL'ARTE Antoine Watteau. Pierrot. 1718. Louvre Museum, Paris, France.

145 NOBODY'S FOOL Theodoor Rombouts. A Card Player Showing His Hand. c. 1616-1637, oil on canvas. Private collection.

149 NASTY WOMAN John Everett Millais. Joan of Arc. 1865. London, Royal Academy of Arts, London, England.

151 L'ENFANT TERRIBLE William Adolph Bouguereau. Meditation. 1885, oil on canvas. Joslyn Art Museum, Omaha, NE, USA.

153 COVER GIRL Norman Rockwell. Girl Reading The Post. Cover of The Saturday Evening Post, March 1, 1941.

155 STATE OF EMERGENCY René Magritte. Portrait. 1935. Museum of Modern Art, New York, NY, USA.

157 DON'T SHOOT THE MESSENGER Kazimir Malevich. Black Square. c. 1930, oil on canvas. Hermitage, Saint Petersburg, Russia.

161 ET TU, BOLTON? Étienne-Jean Delécluze. The Emperor Augustus Rebuking Cornelius Cinna for His Treachery. 1781–1863. The Bowes Museum, Barnard Castle, Co., Durham, UK.

163 CLOAK AND DAGGERS Jean-Auguste-Dominique Ingres. Portrait of François-Maurius Granet. 1809, oil on canvas. British Museum of Art, London, England.

165 MARY, MARY, QUITE CONTRARY Angelo Bronzino. Portrait of Laura Battiferri. c. 1560, oil on canvas. Palazzo Vecchio, Florence, Italy.

167 PITCH PERFECT Edgar Degas. Singer with a Glove. 1878, pastel on canvas. Harvard Museum, Cambridge, MA, USA.

169 ALL THE RAGE Norman Rockwell. Portrait of a Coal Miner. 1948. Norman Rockwell Museum, Stockbridge, MA, USA.

173 LAW AND DISORDER René Magritte. The Month of Harvest of the Grape. 1959, oil on canvas. Private collection.

175 DOLLARS AND SENSE René Magritte. La Grande Guerre (The Great War). 1964, oil on canvas. Private collection.

177 LOCATION, LOCATION, LOCATION Edward Hopper. Western Motel. 1957, oil on canvas. Yale University Art Gallery, New Haven, CT, USA.

179 DRINKING PROBLEM René Magritte. Homme Assis à une Table (Man Seated at Table). 1960, gouache and pencil on paper. Private collection.

181 HARD SELL Elizabeth I (Armada Portrait). George Gower. 1588, oil on oak panel. Woburn Abbey, Bedfordshire, England.

183 ETCHED IN STONE Sir Henry Raeburn. Reverend Robert Walker. Skating on Duddingston Loch. c. 1790, oil on canvas. National Gallery of Scotland.

185 GO FUND ME Giorgio Vasari. Portrait of Lorenzo de' Medici. c. 1533–1534, tempera on panel. Uffizi Gallery, Florence, Italy.

187 PARDON ME Carl Gutherz. Portrait of Susan B. Anthony. 1895, oil on canvas. National Portrait Gallery, Smithsonian, Washington, D.C., USA.

189 NO TRUTH WITHOUT RUTH René Magritte. Philosophy in the Bedroom. 1947.

193 THE ART OF DENIAL René Magritte. La Vengeance. c. 1938–1939, gouache on paper.

194-195 TIME IN A BOTTLE Alexandre Cabanel. The Birth of Venus. 1875. Metropolitan Museum of Art, New York, NY, USA.

197 DIRTY MARTINI René Magritte. Rape. 1934, oil on canvas. Museum of Modern Art, New York, NY, USA.

199 LOCKED AND LOADED Jean Auguste Dominique Ingres. The Valpinçon Bather. 1808, oil on canvas. Louvre Museum, Paris, France.

201 $YMPATHY FOR THE DEVIL Monna Vanna, or Nude Mona Lisa. Salai (Gian Giacomo Caprotti). 1515. Louvre Museum, Paris, France.

203 DO THE MATH John Everett Millais. Ophelia. 1851–1852. Tate Museum, London, England.

207 SUIT UP Joseph Christian Leyendecker. Fitted for a Suit. Oil on canvas. The Saturday Evening Post cover study, April 15, 1916.

209 PLAN A Norman Rockwell. Kansas City Spirit (with John Atherton). 1951. Hallmark Art Collection, Kansas City, MO, USA.

211 THAT'S THE TICKET Joseph Christian Leyendecker. George Washington on Horseback. Saturday Evening Post Cover, July 2, 1927.

213 BETWEEN A ROCK AND A HARD PLACE René Magritte. La Bataille de l'Argonne (The Battle of the Argonne). 1959, oil on canvas. Menil Collection, Houston, TX, USA.

215 FROM SEA TO SHINING SEA René Magritte. Le Miroir Invisible (The Invisible Mirror). 1942, oil on canvas. Private collection.

217 THAT'S DEBATABLE René Magritte. Le Présent (The Present). 1939, gouache on paper. Private collection.

219 LIVE AND LET DIE René Magritte. The Looking Glass. 1963, oil on canvas. Menil Collection, Houston, TX, USA.

221 RECALCULATING Unkown. The Allegorical Portrait of Elizabeth I. 1610. Corsham Court, Wiltshire, England.

223 REIN IN DELUSIONS René Magritte. Le Chant de l'Orage (Song of the Storm). 1951. Menil Collection, Houston, TX, USA.

225 THE PUNTER J.C. Leyendecker. Football Kickoff. Saturday Evening Post, November 14, 1908.

227 BYE DON Grant Woods. American Gothic. 1930, oil on composition board. Whitney Museum, New York, NY, USA.

BOOK REVIEWS

Art 101 of the Deal:
Donald J. Trump Off the Wall

MIKE, Museum Director, Educator
★★★★★
Give Us More!
These are difficult times. and this is the life preserver you
need to keep your head above water. Cathy Hull takes on the
president with a satirist's rapier wit and a creative ability to
make old master paintings explain the world to us in new
ways. In this handsomely produced book, her bite is even more
dangerous than her bark. In page after page, she skewers him
and pins his craziness to the page. Each exquisitely crafted
image gives us layer upon layer of things to think about, at the
same time prompting a huge YES.

Cathy Hull — more please! We desperately need help to
navigate the next months too.

M. Thomson, author, *Dreaming of Oranges*
★★★★★
Superb Satire
Hull ranks among the very best of satirists through the ages.
This is a masterpiece.

Paint Book, Florence Janovic Author, *The Hospital
Experience: A Guide for Patients and Their Families*
★★★★★
Something Worth Having Now
It's hard to find something to laugh about right now but if you
love, art, decency, democracy you'll love Cathy Hull's masterful
new book, *Art 101 of the Deal: Donald J. Trump off the Wall.*
And you've got the time to read and enjoy and share it.

ABOUT THE AUTHOR

Zeitgeist B.C. (before coronavirus)

*"If I could say it in words,
there would be no reason to paint."*
—EDWARD HOPPER

Author/illustrator Cathy Hull has always viewed and depicted the world, politics, and current events through the lens of art history. Decades before the stimulating creative art challenges, the pandemic, lockdowns, Zoom calls, and virtual happy hours; the artist — inspired by the masters — began juxtaposing incongruous icons and symbols in familiar settings to convey striking comparisons. We might have progressed from cave drawings to emojis, but images — universal and constant across human history — still do more than just literally represent an idea.

Creatives are no strangers to self-isolation — most are now doing what they have always done — working remotely from home. Happily, the internet has made it easier than ever before to relate to and connect with others within this strange, shared but disparate reality — leading to many *a-ha* moments.

A global pandemic and a president that has usurped the world stage demands political visual commentary and analysis

COVID-19 revealed tragic flaws in Trump's character and psychology exposing a self-serving "winning" alt-fact parallel universe. Gaslight.

Contributor's Prior Work
Art 101 of the Deal: Donald J. Trump Off the Wall

Cathy Hull is featured in *All the Art That's Fit to Print (And Some That Wasn't): Inside The New York Times Op-Ed Page*, *Watergate Without Words* (A Rolling Stone Special Project), *Sourcebook of Visual Ideas*, *Crazy Commercials* (Scholastic Books), *Who's Who of American Artists*, *Graphis*, *Print*, *Art Direction*, *The Nebelspalter* (Swiss satirical magazine), *U & lc Illustration With a Capital IQ*, *recipient of the 50 Best Books of the Year Award.

"Just because you're paranoid doesn't mean they aren't after you."
—JOSEPH HELLER

ACKNOWLEDGMENTS

"The past is never dead. It's not even past."
—WILLIAM FAULKNER, *Requiem for a Nun*

Little did I know that a mid-day fire in my college dorm at the beginning of second semester senior year was to precipitously mark the end of my world as I knew it. With Linda Ronstadt's Stone Pony playing on the radio, I reluctantly left my ivory tower clad in a $25 thrift store raccoon coat, Gunther, Dr. Scholl's sandals, and (fresh) underwear, to join others on the snow-covered lawn only to be informed this was not a drill.

Books, projects, papers, clothing, art work, and my most treasured worldly possessions, senior thesis, Independent study art project, comprehensive exams prep, dreams, and my new found resolve to finish college with a bang not a whimper literally went up in smoke. No, not an epic global pandemic; but my own personal apocalypse and purgatory.

Not everyone was affected: no shared shock, fear, anger, grief, depression, insomnia, empathy; no special accommodations were made regarding school requirements in order to graduate. Hyperbole? Perhaps? Not really. They never warned or prepared us for such an event or possibility at matriculation. Life went on; eventually so did I. What was the unthinkable alternative?

Nothing seemed more futile, meaningless, or absurd than creating art. I was in my Nihilist stage.

Regardless, ultimately I did find my visual voice and a renewed purpose. Eventually, I re-charted a course, and, with great trepidation, reinvented myself. And so it began. Again.

As we shelter in place, I now obsess and stress about Gen Z and their loss of innocence and traditions — no proms, graduations, finals, classes, mundane interactions with friends, no closure; all the rites of passages and traditions that mark us when in the formative years, the mile-marker memories that comfort us in old age. No guarantee that colleges will open in the fall or anticipation of leaving home to begin the first chapter of the rest of their lives. Just incertitude. And these are the very lucky ones of means with loving parents or parent, homes, family, and emotional security. Let us never forget the countless others with no support systems, greater struggles, and fewer prospects. They were all robbed!

The promise of a better world we adults wanted to provide future generations as it had been handed down to us is, at best, temporarily gone. Role models, inspirational leaders to emulate, a firm foundation to build on, democracy in its ideal form. Vanished. I, for one, am convinced the future is now safer in the capable hands of our kids and grandkids. They will not just endure; they will prevail!

Life gave us lemons? To each his own. Adults cope with "Quarantinis," making margaritas or martinis with a twist, whilst our kids bake gluten-free, no-carb, lemon bars. I only hope you all have a Victoria and a Harrison in your lives to give you consummate joy, perspective, reorder your priorities, restore your confidence, and offer reassurance that, despite current events, for this generation, the best is still yet to come. They never count the days … they make the days count.

> *"I don't know what I think until I write it down."*
> —JOAN DIDION

Donald Trump and the coronavirus have both ravaged the U.S. and the world. Many of us were naïve, arrogant, dismissive, unprepared, shaken to our core by his victory and the divisive partisan politics. He was no longer a running joke; he was now a sitting president.

It was certainly never my intent to write a sequel to *Art 101 of the Deal: Donald J. Trump Off the Wall*. However, I am only human. No artist could possibly resist illustrating the self-inflicted wounds as Trump consistently played to his base ignoring the pain and suffering of the country as a fractured whole and not weigh in.

Truth be told, I surmise I have spent more time *with* and on this President than his wives and porn stars combined. No prenup or non-disclosure agreements required or signed. Admittedly, it took a definite psychological toll.

Sustained by the knowledge that our extended family is safe, we are sequestered, socially isolated. I am blessed with unlimited quality time with my best friend, love of my life, husband, Neil; and our black Labrador(able), Hudson. Life is good.

I focus on my work 24/7. Plus ça change.

I recognize, of course, that this book and my images, even as I draw them, will be ancient history and outdated before the ink even dries on the page. But.

Protest is my cardio....

Cathy Hull
Wit's End,
Carmel, NY
Mayday, Mayday 2020

CPSIA information can be obtained
at www.ICGtesting.com
Printed in the USA
LVHW072014030221
678275LV00005B/71